To Cindy
from
Mother

1996

Linda and Bob Dahin met
the author when they
visited the mission station
in Central Africa, She has
lived there over 20 years.

African Tales

Folklore of the
Central African Republic

African Tales

Folklore of the
Central African Republic

Translated by Polly Strong

Illustrated by Rodney Wimer

TELCRAFT®

TO MY MOM
MABEL C. STRONG

AND HER SISTER
AUNT MARY
WHISNER

both of whom have been an
inspiration to me for creativity
and writing

TELCRAFT®
A Division of Tell Publications
Mogadore, Ohio 44260
© 1992 Polly C. Strong
Published in Mogadore, Ohio by Tell Publications
All rights reserved
Printed in the United States of America
92 93 94 95 96 97 — 9 8 7 6 5 4 3 2 1

The paper in this book meets the guidelines for permanence
and durability of the Committee on Production Guidelines
for Book Longevity of the Council on Library Resources. ∞

Publisher's - Cataloging In Publication
(Prepared by Quality Books Inc.)
Strong, Polly C., 1938-
    African tales : folklore of the Central African Republic/
Translated by Polly Strong. [Illustrated by Rodney Wimer.] - -
p. cm.
ISBN 1-878893-15-7
ISBN 1-878893-14-9 (pbk.)

1. Folklore - - Africa.   I. Wimer, Rodney.   II Title.

GR357.3   398.2096741
                                           91-66693

Contents

Acknowledgments

I am indebted for this book to:

MOUSSA Andre, BISSAFI Jeannot, and the other Africans who told me these tales.
My professors at Pacific Lutheran University who guided me through a Master's program in which this folklore was a major part.
Dr. Richard Patterson and his wife Ann who kept me in their home and encouraged me to write these materials.
My Mom, my sister Yvonne, her husband Norm, my brother Tom and his wife Norma, who have shown an interest in and enthusiasm for this project.
Bob and Kay Ackam who got excited about these tales and made the contact for me to publish.

Preface

I first came to Africa twenty-six years ago. I came to give, but found that I have been given to. It has been a privilege to be taken into the confidences of the African culture, and it is with a sense of respectful appreciation that I bring a little of this culture back to my own land.

I have lived in the heart of Africa, at the very center, where north-south and east-west dividing lines meet in a little landlocked country called the Central African Republic. Its rolling, dusty grasslands, and muddy roads and rivers, have a feeling of home. Many of its foods have become my delight. Its open markets, system of barter, slow-moving society, and even the hot muggy weather have become a part of my daily living, its parasites a part of my blood.

Its people have become my friends, and more. They are my brothers and sisters in a spiritual bond. I can communicate in their language, snap my fingers in the handshake of friendship, answer the vague "mmm" to almost any question, sit comfortably on a low stool with my cloth wrapped around me and pay little attention to time.

At times we sit together for hours in the shade of the mango trees, out of the burning sun, or as the warm night descends, around the thin glow of a lantern and dying embers of the fire. We feel a sense of oneness, but there is also a strange gulf that keeps us apart. At times, vast fields of unknowns slow conversations to a stop because of two minds that can no longer grasp and understand mutual ideas. There are reserves of sacred feelings that remain concealed for fear of misunderstanding and possible abuse. This is both the mystery and the marvel of the meeting of two different cultures.

I come from a world of industry, books, experimentation, and material proofs. I have walked sidewalks and climbed stairs, sped through space in cars, elevators, and airplanes. I think with computers, charts, and calculators rooted in math and electronics.

My African companions have a background of living close to the land: house, garden, family, tribe, food, birth, and death. They walk dirt paths with the full sensitivity of bare feet and a communion with the world around them. They move quickly, quietly, and stealthily through grasses, bush, and dusty villages. Many have traveled no farther than to visit their family and neighbors a few miles away, have read no books, seen no films, and never possessed a newspaper or journal. They think in terms of spirits who are near, who cause sickness, famine, floods, and other disasters. Their roots are deep in ancestry, tribal submission, spirit appeasement, gain by craftiness or deceit, and acceptance in the group. Their experiences of life are understood in terms of body cravings, survival, custom, and mysticism. They live for today. Their stories reflect their culture.

Tere, a prominent supernatural figure, appears in many of the tales of this region. Nowhere is there any indication of his size, physical structure, or appearance. He is left totally to the listener's imagination. His character is determined only by his actions.

Ordinary people become extraordinary because of supernatural powers entrusted to them, or in some way involving them. In Central African tales the style is clear, concise, active, and intense.

Someone appears, or is. A situation or problem presents itself and action takes place. The stories are simple, brief, and to the point, with principles quickly grasped by children or unlettered peoples. The lesson of the tale is generally sharp and definite. Repetition is often used to help both the teller and listener, who are totally dependent on memory for what is recalled and told, or heard.

The tales open directly, and often end with the same abruptness. Unlike the fairy tales of Western cultures, "They lived happily ever after" is not the most common ending. The Africans of this area often leave the situation unsolved. An ending frequently found is, "And so they are enemies just until today," or, "That is why . . . just until today."

So oral tradition goes on, and so we record it, learning to love and appreciate a people perhaps little known to the "outside" world.

It is my unique privilege to have working with me a young man with a keen appreciation both for art and for Africa. Rodney Wimer spent most of his growing-up years in the Central African Republic. As his high school teacher, I watched him draw lions, flowers, and people with a rare sensitivity for form and feeling. His artistic achievements moved to Hawaii and then back to the continental U.S.A., where, at the onset of this project, I was delighted to find him again, working in his own art studio. I know of no one better prepared to bring, through pictures, what I have sought to bring through words.

To visit foreign lands is an excitement. To sample foods and life styles is intriguing. And to live and work in another culture is an education. But to spend the bulk of one's adult life with people of a different language and life style is an enriching experience which merits sharing.

Polly C. Strong
Bangui, Central African Republic

THE STORY OF TERE
AND THE CROCODILES

There was a big water with crocodiles in it. They killed people all of the time when the people wanted to go to the other side of the water. The people were very much afraid of this water.

One day Tere said to his wife, "I will go to the other side of the water."

His wife said to him, "Look, people are afraid of that water because there are crocodiles in it. Why do you say that you want to go to the other side of the water? What do you want to do there? I don't want you to go."

When Tere's wife had gone to the garden, Tere got up and went to the edge of the water. He searched his heart. He said, "What will I do today to get to the other side of the water?" He then went down into the water.

Look, a crocodile grabbed Tere. Very quickly, while the crocodile was taking Tere away, a komba (big bird) began to cry out. He said, "Poor Tere. Poor Tere. Today a hard thing has come to you."

Tere said, "Yes, when I am no more, people will see the last of the beauty that I made on your body, and they won't remember me and the beautiful things I did."

"So!" said one of the crocodiles, and he asked Tere, "Is it you who makes the body of komba (big bird) so pretty?"

Tere said, "Yes, it is me."

The crocodile asked Tere, "Can you make me and my children beautiful like that too?"

Tere said, "Yes, I will make beauty on your body for nothing." Therefore the crocodile didn't hurt Tere.

The crocodile said, "Because of this beauty, I cannot kill you. I want you to make beauty on my body and on the bodies of my children."

The crocodile went with Tere and put him in a sleeping

place in the crocodile village. Look, the eggs that the crocodiles had laid were everywhere. Tere said to the crocodile, "I will make the beauty on your children first." Tere asked them to beat much flour, to hunt much firewood, to come with two big pots and much salt. When they had found everything, they were to put it into the house where the crocodile eggs were lying, because he would sleep in that house so that he could make the beauty on the bodies of the children. Tere wanted to sleep next to the eggs so that he could eat them all up.

Tere said to the crocodile, "Now everything is prepared. I am going into the house. I will sleep there for five nights so that afterwards I will come out. When I have gone into the house, you shut the door firmly so that no one can enter after me because if the door is opened, the beauty will not become good."

Tere went into the house. They closed the door well behind him. Look, there were many, many crocodile eggs. He took some of the eggs and filled the big pot. He put it on the fire. He took another egg and he made the outside of it very beautiful. He put the beautiful egg outside. He showed it to the crocodiles. He asked them, "Is it good?"

When they saw the outside of the egg, the outside was very beautiful. They all shouted with joy, "Yes, yes. It is very pretty."

Tere cooked his eggs. He fixed his food. He cooked his eggs that way until he had eaten them all. Tere tricked the crocodiles for five days that way while he was eating all of their eggs.

The day that Tere left, his wife returned to the village in the evening. She could not find Tere, her husband. Tere's wife asked the children and they said to her, "We saw our father. He passed by the way to the water." When Tere did not return the next day they thought that he had died. After a few more days they were sure they would never see him again.

After five days, Tere came out of the crocodile's house. He said to the crocodile, "Now I have made pretty the outside of all the eggs. Look, the things that I use to make things pretty, are all gone. I want you to take me to the other side of the water so that I can hunt for some more things of beauty, to put beauty on you, your wife, and your older children. When I have gone, I don't want one person to open the door of the house after me. I want it to remain closed until I return."

The crocodile agreed. He took Tere, and they started out for the other side of the water. The face of the water was very great. When they were nearing the other side, look, a big child of the crocodile wanted to see the pretty things that Tere had put on the outside of the eggs of his father. He opened the door of the house a little. He saw in the house where the eggs had been. Look, only shells were scattered all over the ground. His heart broke. He opened the door wide. He shouted, "Brothers, come, see. This man has eaten all the eggs. You run quickly after father so that he can kill him."

When the crying and shouting rose very much after the crocodile and Tere, the crocodile wanted to know the reason for this noise.

But Tere tricked him; he said, "The children tell you to go quickly with me so that I can return to fix their bodies too." The crocodile thought Tere was telling him the truth. He went quickly with Tere to the other side of the water. As they approached the far shore, look, one of the children of the crocodile was chasing them. He came near to them. Look, they had already reached the other side. Tere got off the crocodile's back.

The child cried out, "Father, grab him. He has eaten all the eggs." The crocodile went to grab Tere, but he was already out of the water and gone on his way.

Tere returned to his house. Look, he was still alive, and he came with some crocodile eggs for his children. Many people gathered to see Tere because they thought the crocodiles had already killed him. Tere told them all the things that the crocodiles had done for him. He showed them also the way that he had tricked the crocodiles so that he remained alive. He showed the people the crocodile eggs that he had come with in his sack for his children.

When the people saw the crocodile eggs they said, "Tere is a man of much cleverness."

The crocodile returned. He went into the house to see the eggs. "Oh! Oh!" he said. "What foolish thing have I done? Why did I not kill that man so that he would not have eaten all my eggs like this." They all cried. They were very sad.

Because of these words the crocodiles say, "Now when I see a man, I cannot leave him in peace." It is because of this that the crocodiles do not want to see a man's face, just until today.

THE PORCUPINES AND THE WAR ANTS

The porcupines had cut grass for their houses. They had put it in the sun to dry. One day they went to tie it into bundles. Look, the ants had eaten it all up. While they stood there looking at it and talking about what had happened, one of these white ants, or termites, bit the hand of one of the porcupines and made a cut. The porcupine shook his hand, and a bit of blood flew up and fell on a butterfly.

When the butterfly saw the drop of blood, he flew up quickly. A big bird saw the blood on the butterfly. It frightened him, and he and the other birds rose up with a loud cry. These birds always flew about six or eight together. Now they flew off together, and they all cried out.

Some monkeys were in a tree nearby. They were eating the fruit of the tree. When they heard the cry of the birds, they thought that there must be a war. They all jumped up to run away. As they were running, an elephant came along to get a drink in the stream beneath the tree. The monkeys were causing the tree to shake violently, and some of the fruit fell to the ground. One fruit fell and hit the head of the elephant. Now the elephant rose up, startled.

The elephant began to run too. He ran out of the woods and into the high grass.

While the elephant was running, he stepped on a turtle. The turtle's shell broke, and fire came out. The fire fell into the big grass, and the grass all burned up. The fire burned the houses of the black war ants, and many of their children died.

In the morning, the war ants began to ask the meaning of the big fire that had burned their homes. They wanted to know how it all started. They gathered together, as they always did, and they said, "Let us go and ask the grass the meaning of this."

They walked in a line, as they always did. They came to the place of the grass. They asked the grass, "Grass, where did this fire start that burned all of our houses?"

The grass said to them, "You go—you ask the fire why it fell into me, the grass, so that I burned up in this place." So they went to the place of the fire. They asked the fire—they said, "What is the meaning of this that the grass burned all our houses?"

The fire said to them, "You go, you ask the turtle, because the turtle made it so that I, the fire, fell into the grass so that the grass burned everything."

They went on their way until they came to the turtle. They asked the turtle, "Tell us the meaning of what happened so that the fire burned all our houses."

The turtle said to them, "You go ask the elephant."

They went their way until they came to the place of the elephant. They asked the elephant, "Why did the fire burn all our houses?"

The elephant said to them, "I came to drink water, and the monkeys shook down some fruit which struck my head very hard, so that I rose up to run. While I was running, I stepped on the turtle so that his shell broke and the fire came out and fell into the grass, and the grass burned all your houses. So, you go—you ask the monkeys."

They went until they came to the place of the monkeys. They asked the monkeys, "Can you show us what happened so that the fire burned our houses?"

The monkeys said to them, "We were eating fruit when the big birds rose up with loud cries. They came screaming at us. We were frightened, so we rose up quickly. While we were running, we shook the fruit from the tree, and some of it hit the elephant's head so that he ran quickly, so that the shell of the turtle was broken, so that the fire came out and fell into the grass and burned all your houses. So, you go—you ask the birds."

When they came to the place of the birds, they asked them, "Can you tell us what happened so that the fire burned all our houses?"

The birds said to them, "We were in the tree, and look, the butterfly flew up, and blood was all over his body. When we saw the blood, we were afraid, so that we flew up crying. While we were flying with loud crying, the monkeys rose up to flee. That was how they shook the tree, and the fruit fell to hit the elephant's head, and the elephant rose up quickly so that he stepped on the turtle, and the turtle's shell broke open so that fire came out and fell into the grass and burned all your houses. So, you go—you ask the butterfly."

They went on their way until they came to the place of the butterfly. They asked the butterfly, "Can you show us the reason for what made the fire burn all our houses?"

The butterfly said, "I was having a good time, and look,

a porcupine threw blood on me. When I saw the blood, I flew up making the big birds rise up with a cry, so that when the monkeys heard the cry, they rose up to run. That is why they shook the tree so that the fruit fell to hit the elephant, so that the elephant rose up to run. That is why he stepped on the turtle so that the fire came out of his broken shell and fell into the grass and burned all your houses. So, you go—you ask the porcupine."

They went on their way until they came to the place of the porcupine. They asked him, "Can you show us the reason why these things happened so that the fire burned all our houses?"

The porcupine said to them, "Look, I was cutting grass for my house. I put it on the ground. When I went to get it, the termites had eaten much of it. When I came to tell them about it, a big termite bit my hand. That is why I shook off the blood. The blood fell on the butterfly so that the butterfly rose up with the blood, so that the big birds saw the blood, so that they rose up with a loud cry, so that the monkeys heard their cry, so that they rose up to run, so that they shook the tree, so that the fruit fell to hit the elephant's head, so that the elephant rose up quickly, so that he stepped on the turtle. And the turtle's shell broke so that fire came out and fell into the grass. That is why the fire burned all your houses. So, you go—you ask the termites."

They went until they came to the place of the termites. They asked them, "You show us the meaning of the things that made the fire burn all our houses."

The black war ants said to the termites—white ants— "Brothers, we have not come to make war, but we want to know the reason why our houses and our children have burned."

The termites said, "Ha! We only make war, when we continue to talk like this." And quickly a big termite grabbed a war ant and killed him.

The war ants were very sad, and they began to fight. And look, the war ants killed many, many termites.

Because of this there is a continual war between the termites and the war ants, just until today.

THE STORY OF A WOMAN WHO GAVE BIRTH
TO A CHILD IN A LION'S DEN

One day, a woman who was with child went for a long
walk far into the woods. It began to rain and there was
no house where she could go to find shelter. She went
on a little farther until she found a big hole in a big rock.
She went inside. There was a large cave that continued
into a second room. In fact, there were three rooms in
the big hole.

While this woman was in the cave she began to have
pains and soon gave birth to a baby boy. After a little
while a lioness came. The lioness too was ready to have
a little one. When she saw the rain coming, she too went
into the hole in the rock, which was her home. She too
began to have pains and she too gave birth, to a baby boy
lion. All this time the lioness did not know that the
woman was there.

In the evening the lioness went to hunt meat for her
baby to eat. When the mama lion had gone out, the
woman came out. She took some meat, cooked it, and
ate it.

One day when the mothers of the babies had both gone out, the baby boy began to cry. The baby lion came near and saw the baby boy and began to play with him. He gave the baby boy some of the meat that his mother had brought to him, but because the little boy was still a tiny baby he could not eat the meat. When the little lion saw that it was time for his mother to return, he went quickly back to his own place.

The baby boy drank his mother's milk and he began to grow. After a little while he began to walk. Then the baby lion came and took the baby boy outside. After a little while the mother lion returned and she saw the baby boy. She wanted to grab him and kill him. The little boy's mother called out to the mama lion, who turned

to see where she was. As the lioness looked for the mother of the little boy, the baby lion ran off with the baby boy and hid him in the cave where he had been born. Then he returned to his own place.

The lioness came back and saw that her baby was very sad. She gave him food, but he refused to eat.

Soon after both the mama lion and the little boy's mother died, and now the two babies were without a mother. They walked about together in the woods. They lived and grew up together.

When the boy was fifteen years old he said to the young lion, "Among my kind, when we become big, we must find a woman. I saw a young Arab girl, but I don't know what I should do."

So the young lion said to him, "Leave all that in my hands. We will wait until the hour when the Arabs go to prayer. Then when everyone is kneeling on the ground, I will roar and grab the father of the girl. And you, while I continue to hold him, you will come out with a knife to threaten me. I will then let the man go and I will run and return to the woods."

And everything happened just as the lion had suggested.

When the boy had chased the lion away from the Arabs, the Arab father said, "Anything you ask, whether it be money or half of my kingdom, everything is yours."

And the boy said to him, "I only want your daughter." So the Arab took the boy to his house. When the women and children saw him they were very surprised. But they were even more surprised to see the father. They thought that when the lion had come and they had all run to the village, the lion had killed the father. Now they were very happy to see him return.

The father gathered all his family together and he said, "It is only by the grace of this young man that you see me here alive. Therefore, I am giving him this daughter of mine, and I am giving him our side of the land. He is now the king of the land and I am second under him."

So the people built a big house for the boy and his wife, and they lived there.

Every night the lion came to the boy's house with meat. He tossed the meat into the enclosure around the house so that in the morning the boy and his wife found meat to eat. One day the boy's wife wanted to know who brought the meat. The boy did not tell her that it was the lion who brought the meat. The wife was angry and pretended that she was very sick. She went to the house of her fathers and she said to them, "Don't let my husband enter here until he tells me who is coming with the meat every day." The boy was very sad that he could not go to his wife, so he told them that it was the lion who was bringing the meat. He told them only because he wanted to see his wife's face again. Then he told them where the lion slept.

The oldest boy of the family gathered all the people of the village and went with them to the place of the lion. He was angry with the lion for trying to kill their father, so he killed the lion. Then the boy's wife returned to her husband.

Now the boy and his wife had nothing to eat. They no longer had the nice clothes the lion would bring. The clothes they were wearing began to tear and get holes in them. The boy became a poor man so that his wife could no longer stay with him. He had no family. He had no place to stay. So he went away and wandered from place to place looking for something to eat. His help, the lion, was no longer there to give him food and clothes. He had lost his first place.

My heart says he should not have shown the people the place of the lion. The boy was the king and could have put the lion at his side as his guard. Beware of falling into traps by telling things that may lead to evil events.

ROD WIMER FHG

TERE AND THE LEOPARD

Tere went to talk with the parents of a woman he
wanted to take as a wife. The woman's name was Yinda.
When Tere came to Yinda's house, her parents showed
him everything he would need to bring if he wanted to
buy their child. In that day there was no money. Men
used ankle bracelets of iron, hoes, arrows, and other
things to buy their wives.

Yinda's father and mother did not want Tere to take their child. They searched their hearts. What could they do? What if Tere would not leave the way of their child?

Yinda's father said to his wife, "My wife, the leopard is a strong animal. He kills men all of the time. We know that no one can come near the leopard, even to put his hand on him. No man can touch him. If we do not want Tere to take our child, let us tell him to come with the leopard's whiskers. If he comes to us wearing the leopard's whiskers, we will give the woman to him. When we tell him this, fear will work him until he leaves the way of our child."

So they told Tere to come with the leopard's whiskers.

Tere was a being of great cleverness. He walked, he meandered, he looked, he wandered, he hunted for the leopard.

One day he found a leopard. He said to the leopard, "Look, Leopard, you are not really very beautiful. Do you want me to fix your beauty so that it becomes very great?"

The leopard wanted that. He wanted to become very beautiful.

Tere went to hunt reeds. He fixed a large, loosely woven basket. He said, "Look, Leopard, your body will become beautiful like the depth of this basket." When the leopard looked into the depth of the basket his heart was happy.

Tere said to the leopard, "You sit in the basket," and the leopard sat down in the basket. When the leopard was well-seated in the bottom of the basket, Tere began to weave the rest of the basket on up around him. He wove the reeds tightly around the leopard's body, leaving places where his skin showed through.

The leopard said to Tere, "This basket is hugging me quite tightly. It is really rather uncomfortable."

"Oh," Tere said, "that is the way of beauty, there." And he went on weaving in his own way until the mouth of the basket was closed very tightly over the leopard.

He finished closing the top with strong cords. When it was securely tied, he picked up the leopard, who was now in the basket. He picked him up, basket and all. He put it all on the top of his head. Then he went into the village.

When they came near to the village the leopard said to Tere, "Look, I don't want to go to the village because I have done much evil to the people of the village."

Tere said to the leopard, "Today you will go to the village."

The leopard worked hard to get out of the basket but he couldn't find a way, because Tere had closed him in very securely. Tere just walked on with the struggling leopard on his head until they came to the village.

When they arrived, Tere put the leopard on the ground. He called the father and mother of Yinda and all the people of the village. He said to them, "One day, when I talked with the parents of my woman, they said to me to come with the whiskers of the leopard and then I could have my woman. Well, I, Tere, am a strong man. I want to show them that I am a strong man so that they will give me their girl with no difficulties. They asked me for the leopard's whiskers, but I have brought them the whole leopard."

As they all came to look at the leopard, Tere said to them, "Now, he is yours. What you want to do with him, you can do it.

ROD WIMER FHG

The people were very much afraid. Yinda's father and mother gave Yinda quickly to Tere. She became his wife.

In the way of cleverness Tere got his wife, Yinda.

And just until today, the leopards have spots from the sun shining through the holes in the basket. The leopard wanted to be beautiful, but found himself captured instead.

If you put your heart on being beautiful for your own gain, you too may become captured.

THE MOON AND THE SUN

In the beginning, so the old men say, the moon and the sun both had children. One day the people of the village went under the moon and the sun. They said, "We can't stay outside to hunt food to eat because of the brightness of your children in this place. When we go out we think that we must die because the whole place is hot all the time. So we want to ask you to hide your children so that we can go out to find food to eat."

When the people had gone, the moon said to the sun, "We should put our children in a basket and close them up. Then we will go with them to the water and throw them in so that the people can't always come to us with words." The sun agreed with the words that the moon had said to her.

When the day came for them to go to throw their children into the water, the sun took her children, all of them; she put them in a basket and closed it up.

But the moon did not take her children. She took only rocks that were very black. She put the rocks in her basket and closed it up. She deceived the sun because she wanted to keep her children.

When the sun had come, they got up and they took their baskets. Afterwards they went to the water and threw the baskets into the big water.

When it became dark, the sun saw that the children
of the moon, the stars, were all around her. She began
to search her heart. She went to the moon. She said,
"Have you tricked me? Tomorrow in the morning, I will
go to take back my children also." But in the morning,
when the sun went to take her children she couldn't find
one of them. They had all become fish.

So it is that we have fish today, because of the children
of the sun.

And so it is that the moon tricked the sun. In the way
of the deceit of the moon, the sun does not have children
around her just until today.

THE STORY OF THE SNAKE
AND THE FROG

A long time ago, a snake and a frog were called to be soldiers. The first day they were given their work and their clothes to wear. One morning their captain commanded them to play and to run very fast. The snake quickly passed up the frog. The captain put the frog in prison because he didn't know how to run very fast.

The day of the big festival arrived. All of the soldiers were made beautiful. They wore their fine clothes. They tied on their big belts. They wore red hats and they wore big shoes on their feet. They tied on their bayonets. And then the captain told them to stand in line.

They all did the same thing. He commanded them to stand at attention. They stood at attention. He commanded them to march. They all marched.

But when they started to march, the snake slid out of his clothes that he was wearing. All of his beautiful things of a soldier stayed on the ground where he had stood at attention, and he slithered along with nothing on.

The frog marched just like the captain wanted and had commanded him to do. The frog marched. The frog shouted. The frog turned around. The frog turned to the right, he turned to the left, he stood still. He put his head in the air. The captain was very happy with the marching of the frog.

The captain was not happy with the marching of the snake. The captain refused the marching of the snake because the snake slid out of his clothes and walked with nothing on.

The rest of the soldiers all laughed at the snake. The snake was very ashamed. So the snake came to talk with the frog about his great shame. He was angry with the frog because the frog had brought shame on his head in front of the captain and all of his friends. Everyone was sad.

It is because of this that there is a big war among snakes and frogs, all the time. Snakes do not want to hear of frogs, just until today. When a snake sees a frog, he chases him until he swallows him—all because of the shame that the frog made for the snake in the presence of the captain.

THE LEOPARD, THE DOG,
AND THE SQUIRREL

One day the leopard made a peanut garden. It bore many peanuts.

The squirrel began to steal the leopard's peanuts. He didn't steal just one or two, but he was stealing them all the time. But the leopard did not know who was stealing his peanuts because he had sent both the squirrel and the dog to guard his garden.

One day the leopard called both the squirrel and the dog and he asked them, "Who is stealing my peanuts all the time?" The dog and the squirrel said that they didn't know. The squirrel did not quit stealing. He stole all the time.

One day the leopard went to ask the squirrel, "Show me the one who is stealing my peanuts."

The squirrel said to the leopard, "Tomorrow morning you come. The dog and I will go fall into the water. When we return you will see. When you see the one whose body is shaking you will know that is the one who is stealing your peanuts all the time. He will be shaking because he is afraid."

In the morning the leopard came. He said to the dog and the squirrel, "You go. You fall into the water and then return quickly, because I want to give some work to you."

The dog and the squirrel left quickly. They ran to the water, jumped in, and then they returned. The dog was cold and began to shake his body.

The squirrel said to the leopard, "See, there's your peanut thief. He sees you, and he is shaking with fear."

The leopard asked the dog, "Why are you shaking so? I know that you are the one who is always stealing my peanuts." The leopard continued to question the dog and the dog continued to shake because he was very cold.

The leopard was sad because of what the dog had done. The leopard grabbed the dog and killed him. He left the squirrel as the guard of his garden and returned to his home.

One day when the leopard returned to his garden, he saw that someone had stolen his peanuts. He called the squirrel and asked him, "You told me one day that the dog was stealing my peanuts, so I killed him, but who is stealing my peanuts now? I want you to show me who is stealing my peanuts."

The squirrel said, "I don't know who is stealing your peanuts."

The leopard became very impatient because he was very unhappy about his peanuts. He wanted to grab the squirrel and kill him. But the squirrel ran off and disappeared into his hole. The leopard waited for him in vain. Finally he returned to his home.

When the leopard had left, the squirrel came out of his hole. He said, "I will not quit stealing the leopard's peanuts." He called his children and his wife, and he said to them, "Come, we are going to make our house right in the middle of the leopard's peanut garden." And they ate the peanuts every day.

The leopard didn't know how he could catch them. The children of the dog said, "The squirrel deceived you and tricked you, Mr. Leopard, so that you killed our father."

And the squirrel said, "Because I tricked the leopard to kill the dog, I had better not stay outside my hole!"

This is why the squirrel always stays in his hole, and the dog hates the face of the squirrel. They remain enemies even until today. And the leopard hates the squirrel because he stole his peanuts, and they remain enemies even until today.

The squirrel stole all the time from the leopard, and he blamed the dog, and the dog died without cause. Sometimes events are not fair, for even when the dog didn't steal, he was punished.

When you have two people working, and one is always accusing the other of stealing, the accuser may be the one who is stealing.

THE DOG AND THE CHICKEN

The chicken was going to fix words with a certain family to take their daughter as his wife. When he returned, the dog asked him, "Where have you come from?"

The chicken replied, "I have been searching for a wife."

The dog then said, "I would like a wife, too. If you see another good woman in the family you are visiting, would you come and tell me?"

The chicken said, "Yes, I have already seen the younger sister. You come along and fix your words for her."

So the two went off together. When the dog saw the younger sister, he was very pleased with her and wanted to take her as his wife. He told someone to tell the family he would like permission to fix words for her.

The family agreed to have him come. Now it was up to the dog to go and present himself to the family and the girl.

The dog and the chicken started off again together. The chicken said, "When we go to their house, the family will give us food to eat. We will not eat all that we want. We will only eat the meat."

The chicken gave the dog other advice on how to behave when they arrived at the house of the family.

Soon they arrived. The family killed a goat and cooked it for them. When they gave the food to the dog and chicken they ate slowly. The dog carefully ate only the meat off the bones.

The chicken said to him, "Be careful. Don't eat the bones, only the meat. Throw the bones on the ground."

The dog didn't like this very well, but he did it anyway. The chicken took some more meat. He ate a little and threw the bone on the ground. The dog looked around behind him. He saw all the meat and bones lying on the ground. His mouth watered. When they had finished eating, there were bones and pieces of meat all over the ground. The dog's girl swept up the ground and threw the bones and scraps into the garbage hole. The chicken's girl fixed water for them to wash.

The dog said, "I have lost something in the things you swept up and dumped in the hole."

The chicken went to get washed. The dog removed his clothes to bathe also, but instead of washing he asked where the garbage hole was so he could first find what he had lost. He left his clothes hanging on the wall of the wash house and went to find the bones to eat. Now he could have what he really wanted.

He ran to the garbage hole and quickly began to eat. It was delicious. This was really eating! While he was chewing away at a very tasty bone, the little children of the family came by. They had been walking in the woods and were returning to the village when they passed the garbage hole.

There was the dog eating the bones! They yelled at him and laughed at the way he was eating.

The dog was terribly embarrassed. He had forgotten everything the chicken had told him about how to behave at the house of the family of his wife-to-be. Here he was in the garbage hole eating bones! He was terribly frightened. He jumped up quickly and ran as fast as he could to his village. He forgot his clothes. He lost his wife-to-be.

The dog was greedy and lost everything.

The chicken was angry because the dog had brought shame on him in the house of his wife's family. For this reason the chicken and the dog are enemies just until today.

ROD WIMER FHG

TEN ORPHANS

One day a man and his wife had ten children who were all boys. When they had all grown up their father and mother died. The ten boys all stayed in the place of their father. The name of the first child was Deba. The boys all took wives, only the last child had not yet taken a wife. Deba, the first child, loved the last child very much. He always gave counsel to his brothers so that they would care for their little brother well. Deba did not want anything to happen to the youngest boy. He said, "This is the last child of my father. I love him with all my heart."

All of these boys were men of war. When they heard
that there was a battle somewhere, they all went there.
They each had a shield. Even the youngest had his
shield, which their father had made and kept for him.
Everyone was afraid of these boys, and their name was
well known. They had many things for making war.
People from different villages asked these boys to go often
to make war with them, to help them when the battle
was overtaking them. These boys had received many,
many things in the way of the battles they fought.

When the youngest boy was eighteen years old, he said to his oldest brother, "My brother, I want to take a wife." The first son gathered all his brothers in the evening. He told them the words of their brother and they all agreed that he look for a wife.

One morning, Deba called the youngest boy. He said to him, "Now we have agreed that you go, and you hunt a woman who will be best for you." He gave his brother five spears. He gave him his shield. He gave him beautiful things to wear. The beautiful things were: A red stick which they cut and beat until it became powder. Then they mixed the powder with oil to put on their bodies so that they shined. He gave him a bird skin with feathers to fix on his head. He gave him an animal horn they had made into a flute, so that if something happened to him he could call them with it. He gave him a big knife. He said to him, "My brother, you are the last child of my father. When our father was near death he told me to tell each of you not to eat fish, and he gave me some medicine to keep, so that if we went to a place where someone gave us food, we could stir the stick of this medicine in the sauce to see if there is fish in the sauce. He gave a little stick of the medicine to his brother and said, "You keep this stick protected in its skin. It is yours."

"When you go to a place and they offer food to you, stir the little medicine stick in the sauce to see if a little piece of fish is in the sauce. I don't want you ever to touch fish." Then he warned him again, "My brother, I don't want you ever to eat fish."

ROD WIMER
FIG

Now this last child left his brothers to go to hunt a wife. When he had gone a little way, his older brother watched his back. He cried, and called to him, "Brother, our father has left us, and you want to leave us too?" They all cried. They left him on the road to go. After he had gone, the face of the firstborn continued to watch the way he had gone.

Day by day the oldest brother sat at a distance. He cocked his ear all the time to see if he could hear the flute, so that he could go quickly to see what had happened to their brother. At night he did not sleep well, and told his brothers to always keep near as they waited for the return of their brother.

When the young boy had gone, he came to a village and found a young girl. The father of the girl had died, and only her mother remained. The work of this girl's mother was to roast salt that long ago our ancestors cooked in their food. All the time she went to hunt a certain tree in the woods which she would cut to get the salt.

When the boy came near, the mother of this girl saw him. He was very beautiful in her eyes. So much so that the mother did not want this young man to take her daughter, but she wanted the man to take only her, a widow, as his wife.

But the heart of the boy loved only the daughter, and

the heart of the daughter loved the young man. The boy told his woman, "In the day that my father was near death, he told us, his children, not ever to eat fish. He said that the day we ate it we would die. I tell you this so that you can guard my food, so that a little piece of fish does not fall into it—if you love me."

The girl told this to her mother. In the morning, the mother said to this young man, "You and your woman go out and cut my salt tree. I will stay in the village to fix food for you."

The mother of the girl searched her heart and thought, this young man is not for my daughter. I will do everything so that he will want me as his wife. This woman fixed good food, she fixed her body beautifully, and she fixed her house so it was pretty—she fixed everything well so that this young man would want her.

In the evening when they returned, the woman gave food to them. When she put the food on the ground in front of them, the boy took the little stick that he kept in his hair and stirred it in the sauce, watching it. It did not change. He and his woman ate.

When they had eaten, the woman came and sat near to the young man. She said to him, "See, my daughter is still very little. She is not old enough to take a husband. So I do not want you to take her, but take only me as your wife."

As the young man heard these words, he felt very sad. He wanted only the daughter, and he refused the words of the mother. The daughter also refused the words of her mother. When the mother of the girl saw that the young man had refused her, her heart found much sadness and she looked for a way to do evil to the boy.

One morning, when the boy and the girl had gone after salt, the woman fixed food but she also put pieces of fish in the sauce. When they returned in the evening, the woman gave them the food. Before they ate the food, they boy stirred the little stick of his in the sauce and saw little pieces of fish stuck to the sides of the stick. He showed this to his woman. When the girl saw this she became very upset. She got up, dumped the food out on the ground, and fixed some different food for her man. In the evening the daughter spoke strongly to her mother, telling her not to do an evil thing like this again.

In the morning, when they had gone to cut salt, the woman said, "I will be very clever. I will crush the pieces of fish so that it becomes powder so that the boy cannot know." She took pieces of fish and crushed them until they became powder. Then she took the fish powder and put it in the sauce she had fixed for the young man.

When the young man and the daughter returned in the evening, the woman gave them food. Before he ate, the young man stirred the little stick in the sauce and again he saw fish stuck to the sides of it. The spirit of the young man moved in him and he wanted to die. He saw the food and he wanted to eat it. His woman grabbed his hand and threw the food on the ground. She went out and fixed some different food for him. Again, she spoke firmly to her mother, but the heart of her mother had hardened. She was fixed in her heart to do evil to the boy because he had refused her.

In the morning they went out again. And when they returned in the late afternoon, the mother again gave him food. The boy did as he always did. And again he found pieces of fish in the sauce, but he didn't say anything to his woman, who wasn't watching him. He took the food and ate, then took and ate more. His woman thought her mother had fixed some good food. The girl ate the food with happiness because her man was eating the food.

Then, when the young man was finished eating he sat still. His woman asked him, "Why are you sitting still? What are you thinking?"

The young man said to his woman, "I have seen my father, and I am going after him." When the young girl heard these words, she fell on the ground and began to cry. The young man said to her, "You go draw water and bring it to me. I want to wash." When the girl had gone to draw the water, the young man went out with his little hoe and dug a grave, sweeping it out well. When his woman came with the water he washed himself well, then took the beautiful red oil that his brother had given him and covered his body with it. He tied the bird skin and feathers on his head. From his sack he took to him his spears and flute. When he had taken these things for his body, he said goodbye to the mother and then to his woman. They did not know what he was doing. He came and sat in the place he had cut for his grave.

He said to his woman, "See, I came to take you as my wife. I told you that our tribe did not eat fish. Your mother knew these words well. She gave me fish, and I have eaten. Now I am going after my father. See, my father is waiting for me. When my brothers come, you tell them these words."

The young man stood up now. See how beautiful he is. When his woman saw everything that her man did, she cried hard. The young man began to call his older brother with the flute, in such a way that he would know he had eaten fish and was dying.

Deba, the first born heard the calling of their brother. He shouted, calling the rest of the brothers. He told them that their youngest brother would not remain alive, and said, "Come! We will run fast to come to the place where he is calling." They all were sad and took their things of war. They ran hard to find him. They ran until they were tired and stopped to rest. Again they heard the sound of the youngest brother's flute. Their brother was now down to his chest in the ground. The brothers started again toward the sound of the flute. When they came to the village their brother was now deeper in the ground with only his head remaining out. The brothers hurried to grab him, but just before they came to him his whole body was under ground. When he was under the ground, he still spoke to his brothers with the flute.

The brothers heard the flute tell them how the evil had come to their youngest brother and their hearts rose with sadness. They wanted to make war with the people of the village.

A large, old woman was in the village. She was cutting new leaves. She raised them up to them, a sign of peace. One by one they put their war weapons on the ground and sat down. Peace reigned. No one spoke. Only the flute of the young man continued to speak under the ground, he could not close his heart. His flute told the brothers to rise up and make war, but the large, old woman remained near among them. She waved the new leaves high above, among them. She shouted and said, "Peace be among you." And they continued to sit, and peace reigned.

Then an old man said to them, "My children, I don't know where you have come from. I plead with you so that your sadness does not overcome you. I will sit still. You will hear what this girl has to say to you."

They gathered themselves together in one place. The girl went over to them and said, "My men, look, your brother came for me. My mother did not want your brother to take me. She wanted your brother to take only her. Because of this, my mother gave fish to my man so that my man has gone. Therefore, I do not want to remain in the house of my mother. If you wish, I will go with you, so that if one of you wants me, he will take me as his wife in the place of your brother."

When they heard these words their hearts returned to happiness. But they waited to hear the voice of the oldest. Their oldest brother, Deba, got up. He gave thanks to the large, old woman and he accepted the words of the girl.

After the oldest brother had spoken, they all picked up their things of war and tied them on to themselves, and the girl gathered up her belongings. And she went up with the brothers of her man, going with them to where they lived.

From this it is to be learned, that when a girl is born, it is another who will take her.

You, mother of girls, when the man of your daughter is very beautiful, don't let your heart go after him, so that you will not do like this evil woman.

RoD WIMER FHG

THE STORY OF TERE AND GBONGOSSO

A long time ago there was no water. People couldn't find water to drink. Gbongosso had closed the way of all the water. Only he himself had water to drink. When he went wandering around and became thirsty, he went to a place where there was water under the ground. He was the only one who knew the way, because he was the master of the waters.

When he came to a certain place he would say, "Water of Gbongosso, you come out," and the water would come out for him to drink. When he was finished drinking he would say, "Water of Gbongosso, you return," and

the water would return to its place. Gbongosso did this all the time.

One day, Tere went and hid himself where Gbongosso went when he was going to drink water. When thirst had overtaken Gbongosso, he went faster and ran to the place of water. Tere went after him, and, look, Gbongosso was drinking water. Tere came very close, secretly, to know the way that Gbongosso was getting his water. Tere heard Gbongosso call out, "Water of Gbongosso, you come out." Look, the water came out and he drank. Then he said, "Water of Gbongosso, you return," and the water returned, just like he said. Tere now knew the way Gbongosso got his water.

When Gbongosso had gone, Tere came and called the water like Gbongosso had called the water. Tere said, "Water of Gbongosso, you come out," and the water came out. Tere drank. He put some in a gourd to take back with him to the village. Before he left he said, "Water of Gbongosso, you return," and the water returned. Tere went there all the time, after Gbongosso, and he was able to drink every time.

One day Tere came and said, "Why do I only call the water in the name of my brother?" So he went and said, "Water of Gbongosso, you come out," and the water came out. After he had drunk, he said, "Water of Tere, you return to your place," and the water refused to return to its place. And, look, much water came out and covered the whole area, and the water began to flow in all directions.

———————————

Only in the way of cleverness and trickery of Tere, water went everywhere. If Tere had not done this, people could not find water. The water would only be Gbongosso's.

THE STORY OF BAA-OUE –
THE FATHER OF FIRE

In the long ago, there was no fire. Only Baa-oue was fire. At night, it was very dark. Man could not walk, because it was so very dark.

Baa-oue slept in a cave in a rock. At night he came out and sat at the head of the rock, which was high up so the people could see his fire. Baa-oue wore fire on his body like clothes, and the fire did not burn him.

ROD WIMER FHG

One day Baa-oue came to the village at night, and the people chased him to grab him so that they could receive fire, but he ran among the people and his fire burned the people in many ways. The people chased him without success, and he returned to his place on the big rock, the rock in which he slept.

Baa-oue was like this all the time, and there was not one man who could grab him. One day, Tere came. He sat in the shade of the big rock where Baa-oue was inside sleeping. Tere cried, and he said, "Relative of mother, his name is Baa-oue. He has been lost for a long time—dead we think. My mother still seeks him futilely. She cannot find him. What can I do to see this relative of my mother?" Tere shouted and cried much.

Baa-oue heard all of this and came out of the hole in the rock. He saw Tere. Fire covered the whole body of Baa-oue. He asked Tere, "Where have you come from?"

Tere said, "I am looking for my mother's relative whose name is Baa-oue. I have hunted for him all over the earth, in every place. I did not find him."

Baa-oue answered and asked Tere, "What is your name?"

Tere said, "My name is Gbii-oue (that is to say, truth)."

When Baa-oue heard the name of Tere, he came near him and greeted Tere, and the fire that was in his hand burned Tere, but Tere did not cry. When Baa-oue saw that the fire burned Tere but he did not cry, he said,

ROD WIMER FHG

"Certainly this is the son of my relative." He took the fire from his body and put it on the ground, and held Tere around the neck, and both he and Tere cried much. Then Baa-oue and Tere entered into the hole in the rock where Baa-oue slept. Baa-oue said to Tere, whom he thought was named Gbii-oue, "Certainly you are my relative, because your name is like my name." He said more to Tere, "This is as you want. You will stay with me here in the cave in this rock."

Tere agreed. He said, "I will stay with you in this place, because there is no one else to keep me." Tere stayed in the house of Baa-oue, and one day he asked, "Brother, why don't you fix it so that you put your medicine on my body so I wear it too? Look, your name and my name show we are real brothers. Isn't that so?" In this way Tere worked his cleverness to take the fire of Baa-oue. And Baa-oue took his medicine and put it on Tere's body so that the fire would not burn him. Then he fixed the fire and put it on Tere's body, and the two of them went out all the time into the village at night. When the people saw that there were two of them they said, "Baa-oue has borne his son." They did not know it was Tere.

One day Tere made a cord, and the cord trap caught a bird and the bird was very pretty. Tere said to Baa-oue, "Let us fasten a little fire on the leg of this bird to see what will happen." Baa-oue fastened a little spark of fire on the foot of the bird, and Tere said, "Put him on the ground. We will see what he will do." When Baa-oue had put the bird on the ground, look, the bird flew with the fire and fell into a big field of grass that was dried up.
Look, the fire began to burn the grassland and woods,

and the smoke rose up in great clouds, and the people saw the smoke.

Baa-oue and Gbii-oue wanted to put out the fire, but there was not a way. The fire had burned the whole area, and the people came. They took the fire. There was fire enough for all the people.

Baa-oue spoke to Gbii-oue, that is Tere, and said, "Because you tricked me so that the people have taken my fire, now you must make a village for me on the sun, so that I can burn from there. Baa-oue gives strength to the sun, so that it shines strongly.

Only in the way of the trickery of Tere, the people received fire.

TERE AND A GREAT WOMAN

There was a great woman whose name was Yigoro. She said that since her birth no one had fought with her, and she wanted to fight. She didn't want to make words, but what could she do so that someone would fight?

When she tried to start arguments, everyone ran from her because she was an old woman. For her, hunger to fight was like hunger for food.

She said, "Because everyone refused to fight with me, I will work in the way of my cunning cleverness so that I can find someone to fight with me."

The woman had a big male goat that she kept. She took her goat and started to say to people, "If someone wants, he can take my goat, so that I can fight with him." Everyone refused to take the goat, so that she couldn't fight with them. She walked a long way. She couldn't find anyone. She returned to her house.

The next morning, the woman took a different way. She walked, she shouted, and she said, "Whoever wants to fight, come take this goat." She walked until evening, but didn't find anyone to take the goat. She returned to her house. This woman did this for many days.

One day she took the way to the village where Tere slept. She shouted to ask if anyone wanted to take the goat. Tere heard the woman's shouting when she was still a long way off. Tere asked his wives, "What does this woman say?"

Tere's wives told him the meaning of the words of the old woman. They said, "The old woman says, 'If someone wants to fight, let him come take my male goat, so I can fight with him.'"

Tere said to his wives, "I will do it." Tere's wives refused to agree with this idea. They didn't want Tere to take the woman's goat.

The woman continued to shout for someone to come.
When she came nearer, Tere saw her. She was an old
woman. She was not very tall. All of her bones were
sticking out. Her eyes looked old. Her teeth were all
broken in her mouth. The right side of her face was
paralyzed. When Tere saw this woman he thought she
could have no strength. When Tere saw the goat, hunger
for the goat meat made him want the goat.

Tere refused the advice of his wives. He went out. He
shouted and said, "Who are you that you are looking for
a fight like this?"

The woman answered in the little voice of an old
mother. She said, "I am your old mama."

Tere said, "If you are my old mama, come to me with
your goat. I want to fight with you."

The old woman stood at the door of Tere's house.
Her whole body shook because she was very old. Tere
came. He took the goat's rope that was in the hand of
the old woman. The woman stood still and looked at
Tere. Tere took the goat and tied it to the side of his
house.

The woman said to Tere, "Since my mother gave birth
to me, no one has ever fought with me, or thrown me
on the ground. If you want to take my goat, I must fight
with you. When you have thrown me to the ground, you
can take the goat." Everyone of the village came out to
see what would happen.

Tere went into his house. He took off his clothes. He put on a little cloth that he kept to wear when he fought.

Tere came out. Everyone shouted and said, "Tere, man of strength." They all said this. Tere came and grabbed the woman. He threw her on the ground, and everyone shouted over the head of the woman. After Tere had overthrown the woman, the woman did not get up. She stayed on the ground.

Tere left quickly. He loosened the goat and killed it. The woman waited to see what Tere would do with the goat. Tere gave its meat to his wives. His wives began to cook it. The hearts of his wives and children were happy. Everyone said, "Tere is a man of strength."

The woman got up now, and she returned to her home. In the evening the people gathered at the door of Tere's house to eat the goat.

In the morning, when the people began coming out of their houses, look, the old woman was at the door of Tere's house. She was waiting for him.

When Tere was coming out of his house, he saw the woman. The woman asked Tere, "Have you eaten my goat?" Tere said he had. He answered in a loud voice, "Yes, I have already eaten it. What do you want?"

The woman said, "I want to fight." Tere said, "You wait for me. I will put on my fighting clothes and return." When Tere had changed his clothes he came out.

They started to fight in the morning. The woman grabbed Tere. She threw him to the ground. He got up. She threw Tere back down. The woman threw Tere down like this from morning until evening. Tere's strength was gone. It was dark. The woman returned to her house.

ROD WIMER. FHG

Two days later, in the morning, the woman returned
to the door of Tere's house. When Tere came out she
was waiting for him. They began to fight in the morning
and fought until evening. The woman threw Tere down
until his strength was gone. They fought for one week.
Tere's strength was gone.

One morning when the woman came, Tere stayed in the house. He refused to come out. He sent one of his wives to talk to the woman. The woman said, "If your husband's strength is gone, you and I will fight." Tere's wife returned into the house. She put on her fighting clothes and came out. Everyone stood by to watch Tere's wife and the old woman.

Yigoro, the old woman, grabbed Tere's wife and threw her on the ground three times. The strength of Tere's wife was gone, and she ran into the house. She grabbed her husband and dragged him outside. Tere couldn't do a thing because his strength was all gone. The strong woman grabbed Tere and threw him to the ground until evening. Then she returned to her house.

That night Tere called all his people. He told them to dig him a grave. When they had dug the grave, Tere told them to put him into it and cover it over with bark so that when the woman came they could show her that he had died. They would say, "Look, there is his grave."

The people did as Tere had told them. In the morning the great woman came. Look, all the people of the village were in sadness, and Tere's wives were crying.

The woman asked, "Why are you crying?"

They said, "Tere, the one who fights with you is dead."

The woman said, "Good. Since Tere is dead I want one of Tere's wives, or one of his children, to come out so that they and I can fight."

So Tere's second wife came out. The great woman threw her on the ground once. She shouted, "Tere hasn't died. He is hiding. He is lying in the grave, pretending."

Sadness grabbed the heart of this woman. She went to the grave and pulled back some of the bark. Look, Tere was there still alive. The woman pulled Tere out.

Tere was all weakness. He had no strength. The woman carried Tere above her head. She threw him to the ground. She kept throwing him in this way until evening. Then she returned to her house.

That night Tere couldn't sleep. He went to ask for the advice of Brakele, god of the past, who talks like a man but whom you can't see. Brakele told Tere what to do. "Tomorrow, you take a big gourd. Make a little hole in the bottom. Put the gourd on the ground. Fill it with sesame seeds. Keep it on the ground like this, so that when the woman comes you tell her to give you your sesame seeds so that you can eat them and get strength a little so that you can fight. When she lifts up the gourd, the sesame seeds will fall through the hole in the bottom of the gourd. When you see that many of your sesame seeds have fallen on the ground, you say to her that you don't want any words, you just want the sesame seeds. You want her to gather up all the sesame seeds. You don't want one seed left on the ground. Also, you don't want any dirt on the seeds. Tell her, 'For your goat you have thrown me down until all my strength is gone. Therefore I want you to return all the sesame seeds to their place.'" Brakele told Tere to do this and watch what the woman would do.

In the morning, Tere did just as Brakele had told him. When everything was done, look, the woman came. Tere came out and said to the woman, "Give me the sesame seeds that are in the gourd so that I can eat them. I will get a little strength so that we can fight."

The woman went to the gourd and lifted it up, and the sesame seeds began to fall to the ground because of the hole in the gourd.

Tere said, "Woman, what are you doing? Look, all my sesame seeds are falling to the ground. I don't want any excuses, but I only want my sesame seeds returned to their place." Tere laughed, "Ha, ha, ha. Woman, for your goat you beat me down until I am thin and weak. Therefore, you return the sesame seeds to the gourd."

The woman began to gather the sesame seeds. She gathered them into a messy pile. Tere forced her to gather all the sesame seeds. The woman couldn't do it because the sesame seeds were very little. Therefore, the woman was gathering the seeds in vain and she fled. She left Tere.

Listen to this story. When you fix your heart to get food, and it means you must fight, the food may bring death to you.

Look, Tere saw the big goat of the woman and he got into much trouble, even to the place of death.

FOLKLORE
IN A CULTURE

A CULTURE SPEAKS THROUGH FOLKLORE

In the wonderful world of folklore, fact and fantasy weave together to give a unique understanding of a people. Gaining entrance into the African world of folklore is not easy. When I first approached this inner part of their lives, the Central Africans seemed pleased and happy, but at a loss as to how to help me. They usually referred me to a *source*, a local storyteller, who has all the village knowledge and lore stored carefully in his head. He possesses the right information and has the authority and ability to present it to those around him.

There is really only one way to learn the secrets of the thoughts and feelings of African people and to hear the strong, strange beat of the heart of their continent. That is to listen, listen—learn to listen—and listen again. This learning cannot be scheduled for a certain number of days, weeks, or months. It comes by daily alertness to every opportunity. It comes through learning languages, customs, expressions, ideas, and the subtleties behind them. Even then, an outsider to continent or tribe can, at best, obtain only a sketchy understanding. But the benefits are rewarding, and there is always a hunger to go back for more.

The thrill occurs again and again when a story is being told. We sit in silence, and people from the village gather around. Suddenly, the teller sets off on adventures and tales, with animated tones, gestures, and facial expressions. As the stories go on, the crowd grows. Women and children press in, babies cry, children giggle and play noisily in the dirt, while chickens scratch the dust, clucking at this and that. There are almost always little fights and squabbles among the boys.

When the noise grows especially loud, the storyteller stops in the middle of a wild adventure and scowls at the crowd. He scolds them strongly and they quiet down and move back a little, but never really leave. In a short time they move in closer and closer again, as if drawn by the magic of the stories.

Stories are passed back and forth from teller to teller. Even the young boys are given their chance to "tell" and the older men nod their approval, or interrupt from time to time, to add an important detail. Occasionally a woman offers her story and she is heard with the same respect. With every story, interest grows. They talk and they listen, as oral tradition is preserved.

As I soak in the stories, my mind is stimulated and new ideas begin to form and grow. I learn a new appreciation and understanding of the people. New relationships begin to open up, and I start to see values in the stories themselves that go beyond the village and into other cultures. I want to preserve and study them more.

WORLD INTEREST IN AFRICAN FOLKLORE

People generally, and scholars in particular, are seeking a return to folklore. They are interested in people as they are, or were, before influenced by modern tendencies to melt ideas together. They want to learn about roots and meanings.

The tales in this book were told by the Mandjia and Banda peoples. Their languages have not been written, for few people of literate nations have lived closely with them. There is great value in gathering the tales of these people and in helping them gain a respect for the stories in light of world literature and thought. In this way they preserve for themselves a sense of origin and meaning, while passing on to the rest of the world something of value.

It is hoped that by sampling these tales, the reader will want to taste more, and become aware of the rich source of entertainment, instruction, influence, transcendence, and literary art to be found in Central Africa.

Folklore speaks as *the people* rather than as *a person*. A collection of folklore of a people is an accumulation of the heart of the people themselves.

Folklore is as fixed and flexible as the people. It both belongs to a particular people, and it floats mysteriously into the blend of other peoples. For years this has intrigued folklorists who explain this movement as a process of diffusion. Elements of folklore are formed and carried about by people who cross language, racial, and geographical barriers. They are transported by travelers, merchants, wanderers and peddlers. They pass through bilingual zones to plant themselves in new areas. They span oceans and continents. Yet, specific forms remain stable as they come down through the centuries. In the tales of Central Africa one quickly observes the similarities and interchanges of African tribes living near to each other. The same heroes and symbolic figures appear with different names. Common taboos and supernatural forces are present. But even more interesting is the appearance of themes and patterns of other world cultures, but in a totally African context and expression. It is this combination of sameness and uniqueness that gives these tales a particular place in world literature.

THE PEOPLE AND THE LAND OF CENTRAL AFRICAN FOLKLORE

The *folk* in these tales are the tribal people of the Central African Republic, an inland country about 400 miles from the sea. Stretched over an area of about 242,000 square miles, this country of plateau grasslands is located at almost the precise center of the African continent. It is bounded by Chad on the north, Sudan on the east, Zaire and Congo (Brazzaville) on the south, and Cameroon on the west.

The country is, in effect, a vast and well-watered plateau drained by two major river systems. Vegetation varies from the tropical rain forest in the extreme southwest to the semi-desert in the northeastern tip of the country. The great bulk of the country is open savannah.

The Central African Republic became an independent nation in 1960. There is little history more obscure than that of the Equatorial Africa before the coming of the Europeans. Written documents, monuments, and other preserved records only date back two hundred years. There is no trace of the great empires that seem to have vanished from the center of Africa.

There are about eighty ethnic groups, but Sango is spoken in all parts as the national language. The Sango language has a very limited vocabulary, particularly in descriptive words and terms for expressing feeling and depth of meaning. It is interesting to note that the Sango language has words for black, white, and red, but for no other colors. The tales in this study originated in the various tribal languages, then were retold in the Sango language. This English version is a direct translation from hearing it told in the Sango language. The English is not expanded or smoothed, to remain as close and true to the Sango as possible.

The old storytellers today tell the village tales in Sango, evidence of the general understanding and use of Sango. However, some of the original is lost where the tribal words could not be translated into Sango.

The tale-gathering in Central Africa is done through oral tradition, with the listener hearing stories firsthand from the teller. Histories, philosophies, instruction, and entertainment are preserved only in oral traditions, remembered and passed on through speech.

The Central African villages are rich in taletellers and listening ears. Tales and traditions are the core of their cultural lives. The memories of the men and women are a marvel. Without the aid of written records they hold and tell unbelievable lengths of tales and lore.

THE INTERPRETATION
OF FOLK LITERATURE

Folk literature, a part of folklore, is tales and lore put into writing. It is interpreted in different ways by those who read and study it.

The *folklorists* want to observe the teller of the tales. They will note the facial expressions, the erratic rise and fall of voice, the occasional hand movements, and high-pitched prolonged tones. They will be aware of the rapt attention of those sitting around, spellbound by the magical tale.

They will be interested in watching how the old men allow a younger boy to tell the tale, offering help as he fumbles or leaves out a detail.

The *anthropologists* will observe the people as well. But their interest will be drawn to the way they are seated: old men and women who tell the tales in low armchairs of bamboo, cut logs, or skins stretched on a crude frame, women clustered together in the shadows of the trees or houses, men standing boldly or sitting in prominent positions, and children scattered everywhere on the ground or low rocks and logs. They will observe where and how they sit, seeing something of the social structure.

As they listen to the tales, they gather recurring themes: pride, shame, deceit, mistrust of friends, gaining a wife, seeking help of the spirits, punishments, and rewards.

Food is prominent in most of the stories and reveals certain things about these people who live close to the soil. They will observe the significance of a young girl giving food to a suitor, the exchange of food between host and guest, and the importance of the mother or wife fixing food that appeals.

They will record the patterns of the tale telling: when, where, under what circumstances, to whom. They will seek to determine which tales are told only to girls or to boys, to inner tribal groups, to adults, or other specific groups. They will become aware of secret stories reserved for special groups or occasions.

The *psychologists* will seek to probe deeper into the inner meanings of the tales and the feelings of the people. They will seek to understand the motives behind the tales and the imagery and symbolism of the contents of the tales. Their studies will center on determining the people's fears, drives, feelings of rejection, inner conflicts, and pleasures.

A careful listening to the tales themselves will provide a great deal of feeling for the inner turmoils of the people. It will help the psychologist, or anyone, to know something of the rejection of the barren woman, especially in a plural marriage, and the loneliness of the leper and the orphan.

Through the tales we become conscious of a feeling of life process, of birth-maturity-death, which in its simplicity controls the culture. Individuals are born into it, mature to reproduce and continue it, and die to enter the spirit realm of its continuation. There is little sense of individual worth and achievement except as it contributes to the total life process. Children are not individually trained. They grow up in and around the village, reach the age of puberty, and enter the group instruction of initiation rites such as the carefully taught rite of circumcision, then emerge into the functions of adult life. Individuals remain separate and distinct in being, but are swept along in the whole of society around them, within themselves experiencing personal battles and achievements. All this the psychologist will find in their folk tales and observation of their lives.

Taken together, these three approaches to interpreting the tales—folkloristic (humanist), anthropological, and psychological—provide a full view of the people and their culture. With the tales showing actions and reactions, the people are seen both inwardly and outwardly.

THE FUNCTION OF FOLK TALES
IN CENTRAL AFRICA

The tales entertain the hearers, record history, teach principles of life and morality, explain origins, provide patterns for problem solving, and give a sense of identity to the people. Individuals of all ages and position in life use folk tales for simple enjoyment and for escape into the world of mystery and imagination.

Tales are for telling, especially by firelight, where the shadows erase the sharpness of the visible world, and flame and embers enhance the feeling of magic and suspense. African tales are told and retold around the village fires: during the long nights of the hunts, in the weeks and months of seclusion of the initiation rites, and in the secure circle of the home. The storytellers wind out tales of tribe and tradition, and as they tell they teach and draw their listeners into new feelings and understandings. Embedded in the tales of oral tradition are the history, philosophy, and moral laws of the people.

Nature, man, the world around man, and worlds beyond—all are a part of man's curiosity. Folk tales offer explanations that appease these curiosities. Going even further than common curiosity, oral literature has a capacity to satisfy the desire of mortals to transcend their mundane world. Though the African tales do not seem to create exotic lands of castles and royal riches, they do bring enchantments to the existing world.

Humor is enjoyed. Tere, the ancestor of the woods, is the object of many of the jokes. The audience laughs loudly as proud Tere is tossed again and again into the dust by a withered old woman who "just wanted to fight" (*Tere and a Great Woman*). But often the situation is reversed and the listeners laugh with Tere instead of at him as when he gleefully rides across the water on a crocodile's back, the crocodile's freshly eaten eggs resting in his stomach (*The Story of Tere and the Crocodiles*).

Animals also provide laughter in the tales. The snake slips hopelessly out of his clothes on parade day (*The Story of the Snake and the Frog*). The frenzy of the porcupine, butterfly, birds, monkeys, elephant, and turtle gives appealing humor in *The Porcupines and the War Ants*.

FOLK TALES TEACH A SOCIETY

Folk tales attract and hold attention with their entertaining qualities but influence with their teaching elements. As far back as you can go in the study of folk tales there are evidences of moral and ethical lessons.

The old women of the village tell tales to the girls to draw them into the rites or to instruct them about childbearing and marriage. The men tell special tales to the boys, perhaps on the hunts, in the gardens, or in other secluded situations. But the majority of the tales are told around the village fires, with everyone listening and learning about the morals, taboos, attitudes, and laws of the tribe. More than simply stating moralistic lessons, the tale is more powerful in its effect.

The tales of Central Africa include myths which explain the universe and its beings, and other tales which provide support for the institutions and behavior patterns of the culture. It is interesting to note that the Central Africans often put a *moral of the story* at the end of their tales. It is questionable whether these *morals* were a part of the original tales or added at a later date by people who have become more behavior conscious. It is probable that the morals stated are added or changed with each teller, or even with each telling of the tale.

Proverbs, fables, and other tales and sayings serve to instruct and remind members of the society of wise codes of conduct. Pride and vanity are almost universally regarded as evil and are often rewarded with sorrow. In the African tales this is brought out through the crocodile who loses all his eggs because he was overly concerned with having Tere make his children beautiful. The leopard is tricked into the place of death because he wants to be made beautiful.

Greediness and selfishness, especially with food, are evils that are appropriately dealt with. Work is praised in the tales, giving instruction not to be lazy. All through the tales children are told to listen to the words of each other, even the words of the youngest child. The tales of this area seem to reveal a strong sense of extended family responsibility of caring one for the other. Promises, pacts, and agreements are to be kept. Secrets are not to be revealed, and magic medicines are not to be tampered with.

Tales teach not only the *how* of life but also the *why*. The events of the stories are wound around happenings both real and fictitious, which provide an understanding of the past. They explain origins.

Folk tales have humankind as the center. The person is concerned about himself. He needs to have a sense of meaning for his life. He needs to make a contribution to life now and in the future. Folk tales create an access to deeper meanings of what is significant to the individual in various stages of development and experience. They emphasize the human feelings of privation, longing, grief, joy, horror, hope, bitterness, irritability, vindictiveness, and compassion.

The tales are involved with these problems and offer possible solutions. They deal with human anxieties: the need to be loved, the fear that one is worthless, the love of life, the fear of death, separation anxieties, fear of being deserted or of starvation, jealousy, discrimination of brothers and sisters, and similar problems. They can be a consolation and guide for anxious thoughts and feelings.

Fear is a dominant theme in the Central African tales, also mockery and shame. All cause people to want to flee. Bearing children is the most important role of a woman. Love, loyalty, and acceptance of wives are also themes.

Rejection is one of the most common causes of inner conflict. Many African children understand this experience as they are frequently placed in the homes of relatives or tribal members who are not their natural parents. Other forms of rejection may involve a step-mother, sickness such as leprosy, ungrateful children, or a self-seeking parent. Class distinction is a part of village life.

There is effort to compensate for losses, disabilities, and hardships. Hunger is real to an African.

Sickness, sadness, and sorrow are universal experiences. The African mind deals with these thoughts on a philosophical basis. He is not so much concerned with the fact that a mosquito bite gave him malaria as with the question of why the mosquito bit him. He will want to know why the mosquito bit him and not another person. The answers are usually mystical.

Tales expand the mind to reach into places and situations the physical body cannot experience—what did occur, is occurring, and will undoubtedly occur again. Space and locality do not limit the movement of tales. They give the listener a sense of limitless presence in all places. In the African tales people are taken in and out of the ground in figures and pretenses of death. They go in and out of forests and villages with little effort. Tere and others go to heaven and return to earth. Sizes and shapes change. Spirits and supernatural people inhabit the woods and bushlands. In the tales, villagers talk with these beings giving them a sense of integration with *other worlds*.

Everything can enter into relationships with everything else in the tales. This is both the miracle and simplicity of the fairy tale. One of the most common relationships is between people and animals. Animals are involved with people in marriage, eating, caring for them, and in various situations of struggle. All this gives a sense of oneness to people and the natural world around them.

The spirit world is very real and the influence and advice of spirit beings is both sought and followed. Brakele, the spirit who lives in the roots of the trees, is frequently consulted. He gives advice both to gods and mortals. He is considered to be one of Tere's older brothers.

Perhaps the strongest integrating force of the Central African tales is the personage of Tere. He is both deity (in ancestry) and human. He is present, past, and future. He appears in many places. He interacts with man, beasts, nature, and divinity. He binds them all together in events and circumstances. Tere is like Prometheus of the Greeks and the coyote of the native Americans. He is recognized as an historical power descending from and associated with their concepts of deity. He is like a fallen deity.

There are many references to Tere in this part of Africa, and in all of them he is the same personality: a trickster, deceiver, and the genie of the earth. He is considered an ancient ancestor of the people, older than humanity itself.

Tere is attributed with bringing to man most of the earthly things essential to his well-being: animals, plants, water, and fire. He is not the creator of these things, but is the earthy one who gets these things from the god or supreme being and makes them available to man. He does not always do this in an honest manner, nor does he do it out of a benevolent spirit, but he is responsible all the same for much that is on the earth today. Some of the richest tales of these people are involved with Tere's acts in furbishing the earth.

Tere's actions go beyond bringing things to man. He is also actively involved with man and animals, carrying out the functions of human life: hunting, eating, marrying, and fathering children. He is always characterized by his greed, deception, and sense of humor. He shows men how to plant, fix their houses, behave with prospective in-laws, treat their wives, and overcome problems. He teaches men the meanings and philosophies of life and death. Even though his actions are not always considered "right" he has the ear of the people. He often errs and is punished for his follies.

Tere is best understood when placed into the religious picture of the people. He is considered as a son of god. Africans are a very religious people. A supreme being, or god, is at the base of almost all of their culture. Though African people are often considered animistic in their practices of worship, outside the traditionally Muslim and Christian communities they are more monotheistic in their beliefs about origins than is commonly realized.

God is usually associated with the sky and/or water. Rain is considered a blessing. He is considered to be supreme and source of all things, but he is not thought to be concerned with the people. Lesser beings, descendents of god who are concerned with gardens, rain, sickness, and so on, are more relevant to the actual practices of African worship. They think that the supreme god is good, all powerful, all knowing, everywhere present—yet abstract and distant. Because he is good they do not fear or worship him, though they may toss a morsel of food into the woods for him when they sit to eat.

The Africans don't seem to have the idea of creation from nothing. It is an idea too mysterious, too abstract for them. God is not God because he created, but because he is the source or cause, the supreme being.

Absorbed by the cares of daily living, the people have looked less toward the sky, thinking little if anything about the supreme being. He is good, but the nature he gives life to is a source of evil. Storms, sickness, and pestilence, are attributed to the earthly beings, genies of the land, forces of nature, that rule on the earth. It is these lesser beings who are worshiped, whose actions directly affect the people. There is continual fear of offending these beings. But often there is pleading for spirit-help for things that cannot be gotten by human power.

In African thinking about the physical and the spiritual, these are but two dimensions of one and the same universe. The invisible world presses hard upon the visible.

Like the Greek mythologies and other ancient legends, the tales of Central Africa are filled with personages, explanations, and unusual events. But like many other ancient riches, they are hidden from much of the world, and possibly are becoming buried, never to be uncovered again.

Type set in Goudy Old Style, printed on P.H. Glatfelter Co.
paper, alkaline-sized and acid-free, with 50% recycled fibers.